JUNIOR BIOGRAPHIES



Kristen Rajczak Nelson

# MAYA ANGELOU

## AFRICAN AMERICAN POET

Enslow Publishing
101 W. 23rd Street
Suite 240
New York, NY 10011
USA
enslow.com

# Words to Know

**abuse** To treat in a cruel way.

**culture** The beliefs and customs of a group.

**divorce** To end a marriage.

**graduate** To complete school and receive a diploma.

**guild** A group of people with similar interests.

**inauguration** A ceremony at which a person is introduced to office.

**inspire** To move someone to do something.

**nomination** The act of choosing someone for a job or award.

**opera** A stage show that only uses singing as a way of telling the story.

**screenplay** The written form of a movie.

# CONTENTS

Maya Angelou

# CHAPTER 1
# HOME AND FAMILY

Marguerite Annie Johnson was born on April 4, 1928, in St. Louis, Missouri. She lived with her parents, Bailey and Vivian Johnson. Marguerite had an older brother named Bailey. He gave her the nickname "Maya."

Maya's parents **divorced** when she was three years old. Maya and Bailey moved to Arkansas. They lived at their grandmother's home. Maya loved her grandmother very much. Maya called her "Momma."

## A DIFFICULT TIME

Maya lived with her mother for a short time in St. Louis. Her mother's boyfriend **abused** Maya. The man was eventually killed for what he'd done. Maya was very upset by what had happened to her. She stopped talking for five years.

**Maya Angelou Says:**

**"We delight in the beauty of the butterfly, but rarely admit the changes it has gone through to achieve that beauty."**

**While Maya was not talking, she read a lot. She learned many poems by heart.**

## BECOMING MAYA ANGELOU

In 1940, Maya and her brother moved to California to be with their mother. Maya went to high school there. She took dance and drama classes. Maya **graduated** from high school. A few weeks later, she had a baby named Clyde. She called him Guy.

Maya had many jobs. She was the first female, black cable car conductor. Later she was a cook, waitress, and mechanic. Maya also like to sing and dance. She married a sailor named Tosh Angelos. Maya needed a stage name.

San Francisco in the 1950s. Maya was a conductor for cable cars like this one.

She decided to use her husband's name. She became Maya Angelou. Maya and Tosh were married for only a few years.

Maya worked as a singer and dancer in San Francisco. She traveled to New York City. She wanted to learn more about performing. Soon she took her talents around the world.

# Chapter 2
# Art Around the World

Angelou had always loved to write. She wrote poems and essays in her journal as a child. But then she went to New York City. Her new friends there encouraged her to write even more. Angelou joined the Harlem Writer's **Guild**. She met many important writers.

## Life on Stage

In 1954, Angelou got a part in the **opera** *Porgy and Bess.* The show went on tour. She went to twenty-two countries around the world, including to Europe and Africa. After

**Maya Angelou Says:**

**"My mission in life is not merely to survive, but to thrive; and to do so with some passion, some compassion, some humor, and some style."**

As a young woman, Maya found that she loved to perform on-stage. Her acting career lasted for decades.

a year, she returned to the United States. She continued to perform. She decided to live in New York full-time. There, she performed in many plays. She even recorded an album of songs called *Miss Calypso.*

## Joining a Movement

Around this time, Angelou heard Dr. Martin Luther King Jr. speak. He **inspired** her to become part of the civil rights movement. This was a time when people were fighting for equal rights for black people. In 1960, she worked

Angelou poses for the cover of her 1957 album, *Miss Calypso.*

Hearing Martin Luther King Jr. speak changed Angelou's life. She decided to join the civil rights movement.

**During her travels, Angelou learned French, Italian, Spanish, Arabic, and a West African language called Fanti.**

for King's Southern Christian Leadership Conference (SCLC). Angelou even got to meet King while on the job. She later said that "he was shorter than I expected and so young." Later that year, she met a man named Vusumzi Make. He fought for civil rights in South Africa. The two fell in love. Angelou left her job with the SCLC.

Angelou and Make moved to Cairo, Egypt. Her son, Guy, came with them. Angelou wrote for an English magazine while they were in Cairo. When Angelou and Make broke up, she and Guy moved to Ghana. She continued to write. She also began to teach.

# Chapter 3
# Embracing Race

In 1966, Angelou returned to the United States. She made her home in California. She began many years of writing and performing. In 1968, she wrote a ten-part TV show. It was about African **culture** in the United States.

## Writing Success

Angelou had many writer friends. They told her she should write an autobiography. This is a book about a person's own life. In 1969, the first part of her autobiography came out. It was called *I Know Why the*

**Maya Angelou Says:**

**"You may encounter many defeats, but you must not be defeated. In fact, it may be necessary to encounter the defeats, so you can know who you are, what you can rise from, how you can still come out of it."**

Angelou poses with her autobiography, *I Know Why the Caged Bird Sings.*

*Caged Bird Sings.* The book told about her early years. It started at her own birth and ended at the birth of her son when she was seventeen.

Angelou became a well-known writer. She even earned a **nomination** for a National Book Award. This was a very high honor. Two years later, Angelou put out a book of poetry called *Yet Just Give Me a Cool Drink of Water 'fore I Diiie.* The book was nominated for a Pulitzer Prize.

## USING HER VOICE

Angelou received many honors in the next years. In 1972, she became the first black woman to write a **screenplay** that made it to film. The movie was called *Georgia,*

**Angelou wrote seven volumes of her autobiography. The final one, *Mom & Me & Mom*, came out in 2013.**

*Georgia.* Angelou was nominated for a Tony Award in 1973. This was for her work on a Broadway play called *Look Away.* Then, in 1977, Angelou won an Emmy Award for acting. She played the role of a slave in the TV miniseries, *Roots.* Finally, in 1979, Angelou helped make *I Know Why the Caged Bird Sings* into a TV movie. She was becoming known as an important black voice in America.

Angelou (*right*) appears with Cicely Tyson in a scene from the 1977 miniseries *Roots.*

# CHAPTER 4
# ANGELOU'S LEGACY

Angelou had gained a lot of respect as a writer. In 1981, she became a professor at Wake Forest University. This was amazing since she had never gone to college herself. Angelou continued writing during the 1980s. She began giving speeches and performing her poetry in front of large crowds.

## HONORS AND AWARDS

In 1993, Angelou had her most notable job yet. She was asked to write a special poem to perform at the **inauguration** of President Bill Clinton. She called the poem "On the Pulse of Morning."

Angelou stayed in the public eye during the 1990s. She acted in movies such as *How to Make an American Quilt*. She also wrote children's books. Angelou won

**Maya Angelou Says:**

**"I've learned that people will forget what you said, people will forget what you did, but people will never forget how you made them feel."**

Angelou enjoys a day at a California beach in 1988.

Angelou speaks at President Bill Clinton's inauguration in 1993.

three Grammy Awards for her spoken word albums.

Angelou's later life was marked by more awards and honors. She received the National Medal of Arts as well as a special award for her great additions to the world of books. President Barack Obama chose to give Angelou the highest civilian, or non-military, honor in the United States in 2011: the Presidential Medal of Freedom.

Angelou didn't go to college, but she had many honorary degrees. She was known as Dr. Maya Angelou because of these degrees.

## An Inspiring Life

Angelou receives the Presidential Medal of Freedom from Barack Obama in 2011.

Angelou died at home on May 28, 2014, at age eighty-six. Oprah Winfrey, a longtime friend of Angelou's, spoke at her funeral: "She taught me the poetry of courage and respect." Winfrey wasn't alone in admiring Angelou. Years of speaking out and writing about the black American experience made Angelou a beloved figure. Today, she still inspires people around the world.

# Timeline

**1928** Marguerite Annie Johnson is born on April 4 in St. Louis, Missouri.

**1945** Son Clyde "Guy" Johnson is born.

**1962** Angelou moves to Cairo, Egypt.

**1966** Returns to the United States and lives in California.

**1969** *I Know Why the Caged Bird Sings* is published.

**1972** Angelou is nominated for a Pulitzer Prize for a book of poetry.

**1981** Begins teaching at Wake Forest University.

**1993** Presents "On the Pulse of Morning" at the inauguration of President Bill Clinton.

**2011** President Barack Obama presents Angelou with the Presidential Medal of Freedom.

**2014** Angelou dies on May 28 in Winston-Salem, North Carolina.

# Learn More

## Books

Favilli, Elena, and Francesca Cavallo. *Good Night Stories for Rebel Girls: 100 Tales of Extraordinary Women.* London, UK: Particular Books, 2017.

Kule, Elaine. *12 Authors Who Changed the World.* North Mankato, MN: 12-Story Library, 2016.

Labrecque, Ellen. *Who Was Maya Angelou?* New York, NY: Grosset & Dunlap, 2016.

## Websites

**Maya Angelou Official Website**

*www.mayaangelou.com*

Find out more about Maya Angelou's books, her life, and groups she supported.

**Poem Hunter: Maya Angelou**

*www.poemhunter.com/maya-angelou/poems*

Read some of the many poems by Maya Angelou on this website.

**Poetry Foundation: "On the Pulse of Morning"**

*www.poetryfoundation.org/poems/48990/on-the-pulse-of-morning*

Read part of Maya Angelou's poem for the presidential inauguration, "On the Pulse of Morning."

# INDEX




Published in 2019 by Enslow Publishing, LLC.
101 W. 23rd Street, Suite 240, New York, NY 10011





**Library of Congress Cataloging-in-Publication Data**

Names: Rajczak Nelson, Kristen author.
Title: Maya Angelou : African American poet / Kristen Rajczak Nelson.
Description: New York : Enslow Publishing, 2019. | Series: Junior biographies
Audience: Grades 3-5. | Includes bibliographical references and index.
Identifiers: LCCN 2018009011| ISBN 9781978502024 (library bound) | ISBN 9781978502918 (pbk.) | ISBN 9781978502925 (6 pack)
Subjects: LCSH: Angelou, Maya—Juvenile literature. | African American women authors—Biography—Juvenile literature. | African American women civil rights workers—Biography—Juvenile literature.
Classification: LCC PS3551.N464 Z837 2018 | DDC 818/.5409 [B] —dc23
LC record available at https://lccn.loc.gov/2018009011

Printed in the United States of America


**To Our Readers:** We have done our best to make sure all website addresses in this book were active and appropriate when we went to press. However, the author and the publisher have no control over and assume no liability for the material available on those websites or on any websites they may link to. Any comments or suggestions can be sent by e-mail to customerservice@enslow.com.


**Photos Credits:** Cover, p. 1 E. Neitzel/WireImage/Getty Images; pp. 2, 3, 22, 23, 24, back cover (curves graphic) Alena Kazlouskaya/Shutterstock.com; p. 4 Deborah Feingold/Corbis Entertainment/Getty Images; p. 7 Orlando/Hulton Archive/Getty Images; p. 10 Everett Collection Inc/Alamy Stock Photo; p. 11 Gene Lester/Hulton Archive/Getty Images; p. 12 Robert Abbott Sengstacke/Archive Photos/Getty Images; pp. 15, 20, 21 © AP Images; p. 17 Fotos International/Archive Photos/Getty Images; p. 19 Marlene Wallace/Archive Photos; interior page bottoms (birds and feather) Razym/Shutterstock.com.